airborne

Mark Granier

For Mark Roper

Thanks for a fabulous reading

Mark Granier

Cruit 06

salmonpoetry

Published in 2001 by
Salmon Publishing,
Cliffs of Moher, Co. Clare, Ireland
Website: www.salmonpoetry.com
Email: info@salmonpoetry.com

ISBN 1 903392 19 5

Cover photography by Mark Granier
Typesetting & cover design by Siobhán Hutson

Salmon Publishing gratefully acknowledges the financial
assistance of The Arts Council / An Chomhairle Ealaíon

the arts
council
schomhairle
ealaíon

For my mother

Acknowledgements

Acknowledgements are due to the editors of the following publications where these poems, or versions of them, first appeared:

The Irish Times, Poetry Ireland Review, The Cork Literary Review, Stet, College Green, Icarus, New Irish Writing (*The Irish Press*), *The Big Spoon, The Spectator, The Times Literary Supplement* (TLS), *Raven Introductions 6* (*12 Bar Blues*), the 1997 (UK) New Writer prize-winners' anthology *What Will We Do When We Get There?*, and The Irish Writers' Centre website anthology of Irish writers:
www.writerscentre.ie/anthology/anthology.html

Special thanks to Anthony Glavin for his invaluable help and encouragement; also to Peter Sirr, and James and Janice Simmons.

A number of these poems have been broadcast on Lyric FM.

Contents

Glide-Paths

Here, high on the sea-looking
east side of Killiney Hill at evening,
you can settle into the glide and reach of space –

a glossed world of sea
swaying inwards behind the hill's shoulder
to smoky towns and mountains low as dunes –

and after a while, sitting
on a granite boulder bedded above the tumbling
scrub of gorse, heather, bramble, nettles, you feel

the uncovetted, fantastic
wingspan of composure coming out of nowhere
to open and air and give you back to yourself.

This, take it or leave it,
is peace, creation going about its business
of recreation, in which one merely and wonderfully

figures, like the white sail-fins
or, precise and patient in the darkening gorse,
spiders weighing the last light, threading the spaces.

A Show Of Hands

Every poem is a love poem,
an act of belief,
sap climbing the stem,
the tree,
veining the tiniest leaf.

Somewhere Between Tralee And Dingle

Two of us stood on a road in the clouded moonlight,
trying to make out what dwarfed the dark fields ahead:
snow-covered mountains or crags of land-hugging cloud.

It's there like a threshold, a place where forgetfulness lifts
for that standstill moment, still coming clear
with an edgy moon recovering clouds as mountains.

Another Look

Taller than a three-storey house,
the steep, shaggy old cypress

in front of my window outdarkens
an off-white, rain-battered day.

Fronds tangle and wave
like seaweed in the undersea heave

into deeper bluegreen. The stage
for nothing to happen is set,

then something, a bird, flickers
and hops through the wind-ruffled ledges,

a blackbird glossy as split coal
lights for a few seconds, cocks

a pared cadmium-yellow beak
and the afternoon breaks.

Crop Circles

The cornfield's gold,
an open book.

Then nightfall, and an alien crew
is tramping ideograms, brand-new

place names that will stay in place
long enough to outface

the slipshod clouds
and withering jet-trails.

Horizons

Lemony sunlight, lengthening shadows
on the low granite wall before me

where a white-haired man in a neat navy anorak
faces ahead, his furled umbrella beside him.

Below, and a little beyond, a crumpling of redbrown rocks,
old wrapping paper for

pale blue stroked dark
blue dark stroked pale

In the middle distance (in my middle distance)
a long grey rusty container ship, its bridge crowned whitegold.

Stationary expansions, richness of each slow breath
clarifying, those hosts of envious old selves

out of sight, below that line
whose curve I can almost trace. The hour

has deepened already, kisses of pink on cloud-tufts.
And the old man's gone,

his after-image a watermark on that darkening scroll
inscrutable as always, though still

open to translation.

Flying Over Dublin By Broomstick

I'd had it in mind, how I'd go about teaching them.
Having greeted them person to person, as much as is possible
for a teacher greeting the gaze of expectant children,
having given each of them paper, a handful of crayons,
with a flourish, rabbit-from-hat-magician-style,
I'd write in bold letters, with pieces of coloured chalk,
a title for them: *Flying Over Dublin By Broomstick*
and leave them to whatever welled up in their minds.

But not much at all seemed to well up in their minds.
"Imagine yourselves on broomsticks", I said,
"airborne, reeling across rooftops!"
"Let yourselves go!", I said. The big shy silence
of their incomprehension showed I would have to pay
for being merely a tourist in my own childhood.

Tree-Diving

We wanted to take off like sparrows
or the superheroes we aped,
careening about on our tricycles,
bathtowels pinned to our shoulders.

But those games left me wanting.
On a road clouded with trees
the only way to get leverage
on the real thing, was by climbing.

I could have attempted those massive,
other-worldly horse chestnuts
but a fir tree half as tall took me
into its many-runged heart;

screened in, tented, at home
in a tight-spun dream-nest, resin
gumming my fingers, a stain
archival and aromatic,

I'd shout sometimes to see
boys on the road below
stop in bewilderment and stare
through me, as if I was air.

Near the top you could hear it creak,
sensitive to the least
whiffle of wind, a masthead
fully rigged and at sea,

taking me out on its tide
above front gardens and roofpeaks,
the sleepy curl of the road,
my whole nodding neighbourhood

set back like a stage prop
that I had pushed away
till I took my absolute fill
of the world, and came to a pinnacle.

Primed for diving, I'd drop
face-first through the splayed
ends of the springing branches,
an Icarus learning the fringed

limits of his aloofness,
whose flight was a fully-fledged
catching and letting go,
falling upwards to earth.

"Cultural Identity"

makes me think of my dark
overgrown little back garden,

more moss than grass, the granite wall
shawled in ivy. Enough space

for the washing to do its line-dance
and, slendering upwards,

a tall-storied old ash
keeping time with time.

A Comet At 4 a.m.

One late last look
before bed, and there
it is, finally, a flared
slightly bigger star
plunging but held,
dissolving in the bluey dark
above sleepshut houses and gardens.
Brightest on April the first,
the day before I turn forty.
Birthday candle, fuse-light,
your failing exclamation mark
will work its way
to the back of the mind,
where I've let in these words, minutes
tailing from the earthly core
of a spring morning, here
on the doorstep.

Dublin, March 1997

Anchors

Enough to know they're there, those rows
of hatchet-faced stone heads giving weight
to their landspeck in the Pacific, that they oppose

the cut of horizons, dark rehearsing waves, the night's
foam-flecked cave: steadily sounding the sharp
silence of the moon's unbeaten gong,

long-winded cries of sea-driven birds, chirp
of languages coming and going
and these lines ebbing. Enough to know.

Snowscape

You slept with the concentration of a child
as if you were busy learning dreams by heart,
but when I came to bed before the dawn
you opened out to meet me like a hand,

or the earlier birdsong woke you up at four
and the still, eavesdropping darkness after rain
reminded you of the Spring thaw in your homeland
Sweden, almost nudging the Northern ice.

I see, rather than hear, you laughing now,
bundled in that bulky coat you wore,
backward-walking, towards a screen of white,
shaping a snowball in your mittened hands.

The Instrument

I woke to someone vacuuming in a nearby corridor,
that merciless mechanical whine getting nearer and noisier,
battering the skirting-boards at every turn,
sucking up the dust to which we shall return.

On our deathday it won't be whippoorwills
clouding the window, chorusing for our souls,
nor banshees nor spectres from a neglected tomb,
but down the corridor, in a not too distant room

someone will switch on a vacuum.

When

When the sky comes down to earth too soon
and we're woven into light's immaculate shroud;
when the black light seeding all our bad dreams blooms
in a spine of smoke bearing aloft the brain-cloud;

when one dies and in that breath millions more
are furnace-fanned to ashes that will blow
wherever the winds rage, burned-out spores
settling, out of the fuming skies, like snow;

when all those seeking Heaven's draughty halls
find the conflagration had to spread,
that angels with singed wings have fled their stalls,
leaving behind the dead to count the dead,

clouds will roll back, a full moon mirror waste
and time do what it always does: erase.

A Blizzard In Dublin

That night the window was full of it
feathering out of the dark.

Next day, a smart blue sky.
The city just stood there, roofed
in a silence deeper than Sunday.

Bright-bricked, tall-windowed houses
looked sharp in the wide mud lanes
empty of traffic. Crossing,

we had to pick our way
over slushy ridges of tyre-tracks,
cart-ruts, footprints, the floors

of collapsed centuries.

A Warm Front

Sitting in The International Bar
with the latest *Penguin Modern Poets*
(Armitage, O'Brien, Harrison),
I am almost keeping my head

out of the female universe.
Then she settles on the far end
of my bench, and her makeup and perfume

is embodying in a dust storm
everything I know of 'form'.

Portrait Sketch

His hand, holding a pencil,
is hardly there. It notes

what the livewire blue of his eye
is hauling in: your face, still yours

but out on its own, tangled
in a one-off casting of nets.

Girl In A Wheelchair Dancing To U2
In Lansdowne Stadium Dublin 1997

In a clearing near midfield
she is tossing her hair, waving her arms,

catching hold of, taking for a wild spin
a new constellation, *The Chariot*.

The centre holds. Big wheels rattle and hum.
Sparks fly from her.

Peripheral Vision

Before talk begins soft-drumming
at the bright edge of something that may
be bigger than both of you;

before meanings escape themselves
playing at hide and seek, tripping each other up
for the fun of those soft landings,

you can surprise yourselves, speaking fluently
out of the corners of your eyes,
a language you didn't even know you knew.

The Walk

for Paula

Five minutes from your house: wide lawns, playing fields.
You could let your collie off the lead and watch her
run rings around herself and other dogs,
tightening and loosening big knots in the air...

Trailing beside the walls, a narrow path
was hedged by bushy firs, mature shadings
of horse chestnut, shivery sprays of beech...
where fresh-cut initials had mottled into scars,
clouded, turn-of-the-century impressions.

We knocked a coin into deep-grooved bark. A thought,
wedged with a sliver of copper, secured the ground
we'd walked on and moved through. Something might hold
if we buried it deep enough in that green place:

a wood-knot, darkening, sinking into touch.

Holding Pattern, Dún Aengus

At the edge, safe on your belly,
you relish the whole island tilting

its dark grey wing. Below you
seabirds patrolling their levels,

above you a lichen-bright butterfly
haloing crookedly. Your face

is washed by those updrafts, the breath
of a marbling sea. Hang in there

shaken free
at ease in the swim of air.

Rain At The Hermitage

for Paula

The tree-crowded park is curtained off in a downpour
compressing all colours, fastening silence to sounds.

The tiny artificial lake is spilling over,
its water "all stirred up, a beautiful rich brown".

You've been sitting there with your dog, watching for hours
in a squabble of birdlife: magpies, moorhens, ducks

and out among reeds a grey heron poised, one-legged,
sighting his beak. Will he go for the moorhen's chicks?

You hold your breath for an age, till he unclasps and lowers
a splayed foot, conveying that long-stalked impossible elegance

elsewhere. You feel a memory take root and flourish.
In the space of a few hours it shakes itself into a canopy

and gives me a way of imagining you, hugged by that solitude,
brimming with privilege, sheltered, in place, happy.

The War Years

for my mother

The war years, Dublin rocking from The Emergency,
and there's you, blooming with wishes perfect and bright,
a flotilla of parachutes drifting down out of the night,
taking forever to touch and collapse softly.

7Up, Torremolinos

The icy fizz numbs my tongue.
Curving far out, a star-bright
arc-weld of beach on a calm
black sea. The universe is utterly
beyond me, but close. Close.

Advice To Adolescents

Rave to the slackly made and woefully sung
(the worse the better); be moody, unstrung

for days, in love with drum-rolls of doom.
Never tidy your room.

Seascape In Clare

i.m. Mary Belferman

A perfect day for it, rain
shadowed the coast for miles.
The islands were upturned currachs.

We ordered oysters and they came
arranged for their own funeral.
We scraped out the frilly half-shells

and cupped a slick taste, briny
as the sea made flesh,
sloshed down with a hard white wine.

For the eyes as much as the mouth,
each one a nacreous bloom, a cool bed
peeled back to the sheets.

In Derrynane Graveyard

The roofless chapel holds
stillness in the swirl
of dunegrass and hard rain.

Stained glass gone, three slots
distil unaltered light,
a trinity of measures

being taken: unbroken
core samples of sea,
headland and sky.

The Great Wave — *Hokusai*

Whatever ocean we broke from –
navy and ice-blue rollers
snowballing spume –

freeze-frames, as the world's
coral-fingered wave
whelms and cradles

slim, reed-coloured boats
(inset with fragile fishermen
bald as pearls) unsinkable

as Fuji poking into
or out of the blue
its frosted fin.

The Liffey Swim – *Jack B. Yeats*

"Nobody creates. The artist assembles memories."

When I found a space between the watchers
on O'Connell Bridge,
the blue wind flapped in my face.

Almost lost in the incoming whitegold, legions
of delicate dark arms
were lifting like timelapse seedlings

and falling like scissors. The old stuff
of tall-storied windows and traffic

banked to each side, new strokes,
a broad afternoon in ribbons.

Ancient View Of Amsterdam

– an etching by Rembrandt

A skyline accumulates from scratch.

Holding under all that air
for the imminent cry of a seagull:

ghost-roofs, ghost-masts –
the hint of a harbour –

then the taller flyweight X
of a windmill, and further off

in the dismantling haze,
three others, lighter and lighter,

cartwheeling across the horizon.

The Slaughtered Ox

– Rembrandt

Light loves to fall on flesh of any sort.
The cruciform barrel-wide carcass of the ox,

soiled by blood and shadow, gaping open
for the pallid ochres, glutinous bags of fat,

was ample reason for the time enrolled
to flesh its afterlife and give it weight.

Hung in the Louvre today, it still holds fresh
though *the smell of colour* might unsettle you.

Lines For The Diceman

i. m. Thom McGinty

Good to know you might turn up
in the frieze of faces on Grafton Street,
familiar stranger surprising us
in something from your wardrobe-gallery,

a walking painting say, holding its own
gilded ornate frame, the face
a white mask, Mona Lisa
in a black cat-suit, cracking a murky smile.

Dead-slow, solemnly careful
among eddies of Christmas shoppers, summer dawdlers,
tourists, street-traders, Guards...
mindful of each sound-proofed step, sure-

footed as an acrobat, spaced in, treading your own
high wire. When we looked
at you looking through us
we took in the joke that jumped – a spark of silence –

eye to eye, mind to mind,
across Grafton Street's canyon of swirling clockwork noise.
You're gone now forever (back
into the box with Jack)

and scanning the quickslow, giddy, sedate
everyday street-portrait – its procession
of invisible masks – the eye misses you.
Old Master, Diceman, conductor

of the ungrooved thought, catcher
of the thrown glance, are you still there?

The Talk

Dim, green-shaded lamps
keep the light low, leave corners
for a little intimacy.
Outside, along the Liffey,
headlights are floating past
in the darkening blue of an evening
nearly twenty years ago,

and I'm in my early twenties
sitting on my own, writing
in one of those fugitive moments
familiar to me even then.
I am trying shape my thoughts, pool
whatever words I can catch

before they arrive
and *my careful sentences*
resign themselves to the talk.
This evening would flow with talk
shapeless and animate, conveying us
to the last bus, the following day.

And in they came, eventually,
scraping chairs, unwinding scarves,
slipping their coats off,
ordering coffee or wine...
and I can't remember one word,
not one.

Only what I was writing
before they came:
As with me
the day will have wrought itself in them.
Every evening
a kind of bafflement,
a need to divulge.

A Soft Day

Blessed be the sadhappy walk in the rain
to the end of the pier and back again.

Praise be to friends, new-leafed and old
and those who've let go their hold.

Hail to the painstaking
good, slow, awkward work of lovemaking

that is never done.
Hallelujah what is hard or easily won.

Patchouli

Essential oil, a viscous resiny darkness,
dark as distilled cannabis.
You didn't wear it, it wore you,
filling your clothes, even whatever you touched:
glasses, somebody's sheepskin jacket, each other.
A disguise for hash-smokers, they said.
More like a signal. I followed the spoor through dancehalls
and wild *Deep Purple* weekends.
It was all those warm, warm women I may have met
who reclined on their couches, murmuring
to come in from the cold, to sit, sit over here.

The Disused Railway

The first time I saw it,
crossing the hump-backed bridge,
it drew my gaze, an intriguing seam of grass

dwindling off inland,
past edged-out housing estates.
I might wear an afternoon out, there, with one or two friends.

Fraying for miles,
but the line never led us to wandering
where a wall stepped in, a high-tide of foaming brambles.

With the unmoved graph
of mountains away to the left
and, after the the station, the reservoir wall on our right,

we'd hunt for frogs,
poking dried-out ditches and ponds, and
stirring and nudging our summer imaginations,

bask on a stretch
where sleepers had gone to seed,
our half-a-mile lives abandoned to any beginning.

What Did You Do On Your Weekend In Vancouver?

for Ronan, Roz, Raife & Ben

Walked with the traffic-stream over a high
humming bridge, airborne

before a strange city, its lives
crystallised, flickering with intelligence.

Backcloth of ashgreen mountains,
tangerine dusk, all the colours of elsewhere.

The voices whispering *you should be 21
not 41* I crumpled up and let fall

over the rail, little bits
of flotsam that would find me later.

Sat in a window in Kitto's Japanese restaurant.
Wrote nothing worth writing, thought

nothing worth thinking, unless it was
"I'm here... here... here..."

(shadowface ghosting the glass)
gazing at the carnival of passing faces,

their tanned legs, their many hairstyles.
When it came down to it, did nothing at all

but come down to earth, in the air,
finding myself at last on a bridge

into a strange city.

Vanishing Point

Simply staring
into the space ahead
is not enough. There is
the traffic of eyes to be met.